BOLD

THE INTERIORS OF DRAKE/ANDERSON

BOLD

Jamie Drake and Caleb Anderson

with Judith Nasatir

RIZZOLI
NEW YORK

New York · Paris · London · Milan

TABLE OF CONTENTS

INTRODUCTION

Why bold? Why not! Bold is as much a way of being in the world as it is a distinctive look, one utterly unconcerned with trends. Our clients take this approach to life. The residences we create reflect their personalities.

Audacious visual choices come naturally and intuitively to us, yet we also pursue them with deliberate intent. Smart, disciplined, decisive editing and deeply considered selections up the emotive ante of each singular piece, spatial gesture, and the overall mix exponentially. We believe in design that stands out, in spaces that are confident, witty, sexy, exquisite, full of soul and expressive of personal spirit. From a style perspective, this point of view covers the widest possible range, as the projects in the following pages demonstrate. We clearly incline toward the modern and the contemporary, but we embrace the classic and the classical as well.

We both see and understand design within a deeply historical context. We delight in the unexpected juxtaposition of the great contemporary makers and how we choose to have them live beside the great makers of the past. Our love of statement pieces, whether made today or generations and centuries ago, is obvious. We also believe that not every facet of a room or a home can or should make its presence known in loud visual terms. No residence—no living space—achieves success by big strokes alone. The flowering comes with the layers, the subtler and quieter discoveries that emerge in the textiles, details, and hidden treasures of each interior that reveal themselves over time. We apply this aesthetic logic to every choice at different scales: nothing overly much or overly minimal, too ornate or too plain, too rough or too slick, too loud or too quiet, too complex or too simple. We prize balance. We adore the potency of contrast, the energy it exerts in setting off each element of a room and enhancing the impact of the combination overall.

The two of us are quite similar in important ways. We share an eye and the fundamental belief that interiors should be inviting, delightful, and livable. We value rooms and residences that are dynamic and eclectic, sophisticated and refined, that marry the timeless with today, and that express personality and place. We both thrill to the power of the defining gesture, and the aesthetic force it can multiply when it resonates through even the smallest-scaled element and details. We share a passion for the elements of design—color, form, light, texture, pattern, materials, and exquisite things.

We are also extremely different people. We both value design's expressive powers, of course, but each in our own way and with our own characteristic degrees of intensity. The two of us have our own distinct senses of design history, sets of references, sources of inspiration, and personal takes on, well, everything. Our individual internal compasses direct our personal perspectives on glamour, curation, and elegance, on where each of us sees subtlety and complexity, daring and restraint. What draws one of us to prefer this option over that from the infinite available possibilities—the sequined instead of the woven, the pale rather than the saturated, the voluptuous in lieu of the sloped or straight—lies in the ineffable mystery that is identity, taste, and sense of style. Our singular imaginations, though, work in tandem to shape the thread of each of our designs. These collaborative decisions form the through line in the decoration that we use to tell the specific story of place and express the particular people who live in those rooms.

Why bold? We love design's superpower of "wow"—and the kaleidoscope of almost infinite possibility it empowers us with to create delight for our clients at home.

G O T H A M
G L A M O U R

Inspiration is one thing. Logic is another. Rarely do the two align so organically as they did in this full-floor Manhattan residence. When this San Francisco–based family invited us to give their three-bedroom pied-à-terre in a just-completed Upper East Side tower the full-on glamour treatment, they encouraged us to push the boundaries, particularly with the color palette and the floors (for the foyers, they gave us a tear sheet that we cleverly interpreted). The classic rooms were so beautifully laid out for telling a story of spatial connection that, apart from a new kitchen, the apartment needed very few refinements. Once we established the design narrative's decorative threads—jewel tones, linear and curved forms at play (many of our design), the rich materiality of metals, lacquers, stones, sensuous fabrics, and fantastic art—we wove them into a nuanced interior epic.

The story truly begins at the beginning. The apartment's front doors—a pair of obsidian- and quartz-studded metal panels that we created in collaboration with the artist Gloria Cortina—transform the elevator vestibule into a scene-setting prologue for all that follows. In the entry gallery beyond, the plot thickens with the introduction of rich jewel tones, captivating textures, and alluring surfaces that deepen the sensory delight, plus lighting fixtures and furnishings that reimagine the vestibule's rhythms and patterns in angled, curved, and faceted guises. Given the limestone building's enormous windows, we oriented the main living area to "view, view, view" with fairly low-slung furniture graciously settled into two seating groups. The dining room takes a moodier and amorphic tangent, with a sinuous commissioned lighting installation reflecting onto a stone-and-brass table and rug, all centered, but angled, in space. The kitchen is an intricate, refined, completely functional confection: lacquer and cerused wood cabinet fronts, lighting fixtures, and book-matched stone panels that reiterate the gallery's faceted theme, as well as a stone block of an island with a carved-out banquette. In the adjacent family room, we thought pink, softer than Diana Vreeland's favorite hot, hot, hot, navy-blue-of-India shade, but still truly a neutral. The main bedroom tantalizes with Lobmeyr crystal, rock crystal, gypsum, bronze, beaded upholstery, leather, and shagreen, as well as voluptuous-to-the-touch textiles.

From the front door to the bedroom walls, the narrative coheres. Forms, colors, patterns, and materials enhance one another in a marriage of bold and subtle, large-scale and small. To think it began with such a small clue: a tear sheet of a patterned floor.

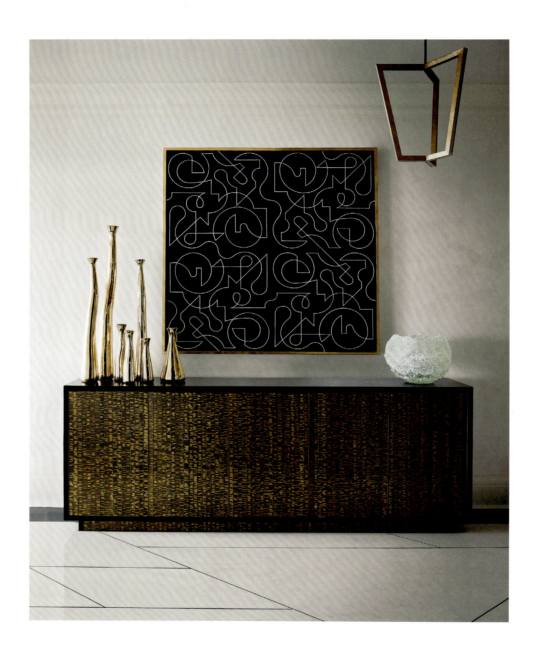

Page 8: Early on, this client voiced a desire for a statement door to glamorize the apartment's entry. A collaboration with Mexican artist Gloria Cortina, represented by Cristina Grajales Gallery, yielded these bronze, quartz, and obsidian confections that, along with lustrous wallpaper and an inset marble floor, transformed the elevator vestibule. **Above:** In the entry gallery, inlaid marble floors, brass ceiling fixtures, and the black, white, and brass palette take cues from the vestibule doors. The painted cabinet serves for china storage. **Opposite:** The pearlescent plaster-finished gallery walls amplify the available light and create a fabulous backdrop for art.

Previous spread: The living room balances organic forms with linear geometries and ethereal pale hues with deeply saturated jewel tones. The daybed connects the room's two seating groups. The pattern and texture of the rug, though understated, make a clear reference to the vestibule doors. **Opposite:** With a chenille interior and leather exterior, the club chair offers tactile as well as visual voluptuousness; the brass table lamp emulates its curves at a much-reduced scale. The painting by Barbara Takenaga comments on the celestial motif suggested by pendent fixtures. **Above:** The custom coffee table rises from a base of stacked layers of lacquer and stone.

Above: At the client's request, most rooms include a desk. Right: The second seating group centers around a coffee table with a sculptural brass base and ebonized sunburst top, an oblique reflection on the orbital fixture overhead. Opposite: The living room's work surface—a custom design with leather-wrapped sides—nests behind the sofa and takes in the city view.

Previous spread: The floor plan flows organically, with classical rooms framed by traditional moldings and casements, an optimal arrangement for developing a decorative narrative from space to space. Here, the jewel tones and geometries evolve from the living room to the dining room. The totemic sculptures are from Elizabeth Turk's "Echoes of Extinction" series. Opposite: The dining room's amorphous rug and sinuous custom dining table take cues from the asymmetrical lighting installation. A metallic underlay sets the teal lacquer walls aglow with a glamorous shimmer. Above: The delicate assembly of crystal rods with brass and fiber optics enacts a luminous drama overhead.

Previous spread: A clear intentionality connects the forms, finishes, and materials throughout. The kitchen's pyramidal pendants recall the gallery's fixtures. The banquette's upholstery echoes the dining room's palette. Subtle welting on the chairs leads the eye into the adjacent family room. The banquette carved into the island elegantly resolves a spatial constraint. **Above:** A sofa built into the window creates a casual TV area in the family room. **Opposite:** The cabinets feature dimensional facets enhanced by the directionality of the wood grain. The book-matched marble backsplash reintroduces purple tones. The stainless-steel hood nods to the table base.

Opposite: An essay in materials and finishes that shine, gleam, and reflect, the powder room could not be more glamorous. Once a full bath, this space luxuriates in newly gracious dimensions thanks to the removal of the shower. The polished marble vanity, sheathed unexpectedly in brass, cantilevers confidently off a mirrored wall. The flanking walls, covered in a very shiny silk, with glass mosaic tile floor up the ante on shimmer. Above: Crystal sconces from Lobmayr echo the multifaceted motif.

Previous spread: Exceptional views notwithstanding, cocooning a room in draperies creates a sexy, intimate effect. In terms of color, the primary bedroom balances the masculine and feminine. Opposite: Lindsey Adelman's chandelier recalls the motif of the vestibule doors. Right, top: Gunmetal beading adds an overall glimmer to the upholstered bed wall. Bedside lamps nod to skyscrapers just outside. Right: The custom gypsum lift cabinet, which houses the TV, harkens back to the front gallery floor.

Top: The main bath's capsule-shaped vanity celebrates the contemporary in an otherwise traditionally inflected space. The unusual edge of the stone counter and base subtly amplifies the vanity's profile; custom hardware and a rock crystal light fixture add jewelry details. **Left:** Silver leaf finished doors shimmer in the dressing room suite. **Opposite:** Charcoal and purple accents combine with silver leaf in the dressing room to exemplify a twenty-first-century perspective on old world glamour.

Opposite: The daughter's room is oh-so-pretty in her favorite shades of pink and bright white. Playfully designed for nights in with friends, instead of bunkbeds, the unique custom arrangement accommodates (even inspires) sleepovers by spinning two beds—one with a trundle, one with additional storage—off a shared headboard. A plush rug, child-sized table, and pint-sized poufs encourage play. **Above:** The daughter's en-suite bath incorporates a vanity that nods to the pattern of her bedroom rug.

Above, left: Quirky and fun, the ceiling fixture in the guest bedroom combines glass and metal disks that tie into room's palette. Above, right: The client requested that workspaces of various kinds be included throughout. This desk, set at an amazing vantage point, speaks eloquently to the materials and details of the custom headboard. Opposite: The guest room may be the boldest in terms of the interior's jewel-toned palette. Upholstered and trimmed in brass, the headboard accentuates its positive embrace of the sleeper by hugging the sculptural nightstands. The patterned rug introduces a luscious texture under foot; its rivulets of gold yarn glint discreetly.

LONDON CALLING

The heart has its reasons. So does the eye. After twenty years in their ravishing London flat, our clients fell in love with this Queen Anne–style beauty. Built in 1718 and long untouched, it needed a significant upgrade. Given its designation as a Grade II listed house—meaning "of special interest, warranting every effort to preserve it"—all renovations had to meet the stringent requirements of the governing authorities, Historic England and the Royal Borough of Kensington and Chelsea. Bringing on a local expert architectural firm helped us achieve ninety-nine percent of our goals, which included stabilizing the house, replacing the floors throughout, and reconfiguring the kitchen for the twenty-first century.

We embarked on the significant restoration in the foyer. The painstaking effort here encompassed both the crowning murals by Sir James Thornhill (1675/6 – 1734), renowned for decorating the inside of the dome of St. Paul's Cathedral, and the floor, which required that we carefully match stones for the pieces beyond repair. This main level featured two reception rooms, both of which we decided to appoint as dining rooms for our clients who love entertaining. In the larger, garden-facing chamber, we refurbished the period envelope—meticulously restoring the original millwork, paneling, and details throughout—and brought the design conversation up to date with custom banquettes tucked into opposing fireplace niches and pieces from across the centuries. In the smaller, a jewel box painted the deepest dark cobalt, we arranged a parure of furnishings crowned by a rare, gilt bronze chandelier by André-Charles Boulle.

The second-floor salon, with its garden-view bay window, practically demanded walls in a shade of soft moss to bring in the outdoors. Here, just as in the large dining room directly below, opposing fireplaces, remnants of this space's original, two-room incarnation, provide anchors for conversational groupings dressed in degrees of lushness, sheen, and metallic gleam, all enhanced by Michele Oka Doner's verdant chandelier, commissioned to bring the outdoors inside. The library, so graphic in chalk white with a coal black period mantel and passementerie cord sketching in the windows' traditional swags and jabots, naturally welcomed a comfortable cluster of reading chairs.

Transforming the main bedroom into a restful dream space, we spun a resplendent cocoon of silk velvet upholstered panels in front of the original paneling to preserve it. Along with their individual studies, the lady's and gentleman's baths, arrayed off of a tented vestibule, provided personal retreats: hers full of shimmer, spirit, and reflection; his, earthier in tone and materials.

To bring the lower-level kitchen into the present, we created breathable space by excavating down 18 inches and combining rooms (the existing division was not original). Then we outfitted the new in lush, visually active materials—richly veined marble, polished and hammered brass, steel, and glass—that, like the entire house, nod to the ancient in the current idiom.

Page 38: The gracious foyer of this early-eighteenth-century house immediately announces its storied history. **Above:** A magnificent nineteenth-century carved alabaster urn sitting atop a custom mahogany base speaks confidently to the scale and volume of the entry and stairwell and proportionally matches a gilt bronze lantern that hovers above it. Conceived as a contemporary interpretation of a classic antique Persian rug, the custom hand-knotted runner was made with traditional techniques and ombrage. **Opposite:** Restoring the entry's original woodwork and period murals by Sir James Thornhill provided important clues for the rest of the furnishings and color scheme.

Preceding spread: In the main drawing room on the second floor, a custom sofa fits purposefully into the window bay, which overlooks the rear garden and floods the room with light. In a timeless mix, period chairs and poufs on coquettish bases help center the seating group around a contemporary stone and bronze cocktail table. **Opposite:** With unexpected niches and opposing fireplaces, the drawing room's footprint is the result of earlier renovations that over time combined two smaller spaces into one. **Above:** Michele Oka Doner created a commissioned chandelier that brings the outside in with clear references to the branches of the trees beyond.

Above: A chaise that lounges beside one of the drawing room's two fireplaces is dressed in a sumptuous, embossed, hand-painted silk velvet typical of the textiles used throughout the room. Left: A truly superb eighteenth-century French chair wears a sublime fabric with a design from the same period. Opposite: Above the opposing fireplaces, a husband and wife from long ago silently converse with one another across the crowded room.

Opposite: A vibrant Japanned breakfront desk nests in solitary splendor in one of the drawing room's more idiosyncratic niches, where a third fireplace hints at the interior's original footprint. **Above:** A contemporary Japanese porcelain bowl, delicate gilt bronze and crystal candlesticks circa 1860, and hand-painted vase from the 1930s atop a contemporary cocktail table express the spirit of living history in microcosm. **Left:** A poured glass and bronze lamp inserts a determinedly contemporary grace note.

Left: In the larger of the two dining rooms, a pair of crystal chandeliers glistens above a period mahogany table and chairs. The original paneling, painted oyster, is a sober foil to vivid shades of cinnabar and coral. **Top:** A Meissen *schneeballen* injects a note of spring atop a contemporary table. **Above:** Hammered sconces nod to current times.

Above: In this dining room, as throughout the entire house, the balance of design history is recalibrated so that a compelling, well-considered story is on view from every angle and perspective. A pair of Baroque-period gilded wood mirrors above the room's opposing fireplaces reflects and enhances the sparkle of the chandeliers. **Opposite:** Nestled into the niches that flank each fireplace, custom banquettes with polished metal tables offer intimate spots for quiet conversation before and after dinner.

Opposite: On the second-floor landing, flanking the entry to the library, an enchanting pair of period Chinese bobblehead figurines rests atop gilded English torchère-style pedestals. The soft, unlined Roman shades continue consistently across all the windows of the first and second floors on the house's street-facing façade to give its public presence a cohesive quality. Above: The pronounced band of brilliant color at the hem of this figure's skirt leads the eye directly into the library beyond.

Above, left: In the library, window treatments that sketch in a line-drawing-like take on traditional swags and jabot with cord and passementerie insert touches of whimsy and charm. **Above, right:** A pair of ceramic topped side tables with sweeping, curvaceous bronze bases introduces a counterpoint of sensuousness into the overall mix. **Opposite:** A circle of four comfortable swivel chairs centered around a tufted ottoman is a favorite arrangement of these clients, who find it conducive to conversation.

Opposite: Excavating the lower level allowed for the creation of higher ceilings in the spaces below the street. The kitchen combines four previous rooms into one large volume where two hammered-brass islands act like parentheses to define additional work areas within the wider perimeters. The lower cabinets sport a cerused finish; the upper cabinets feature textured glass inset into steel frames. **Opposite:** Off the large dining room, a wet bar wrapped in satin brass provides an elegant service space.

Above: A newly installed statuary marble fireplace mantel stands out confidently in the smaller dining room. Opposite: With walls slathered in deepest cobalt blue paint, the room provides a charming venue for more intimate meals. A magnificent eighteenth-century gilt-bronze chandelier by André-Charles Boulle hovers above a mahogany dining table almost contemporary in its elegant simplicity. Gilded accents add more sparkle.

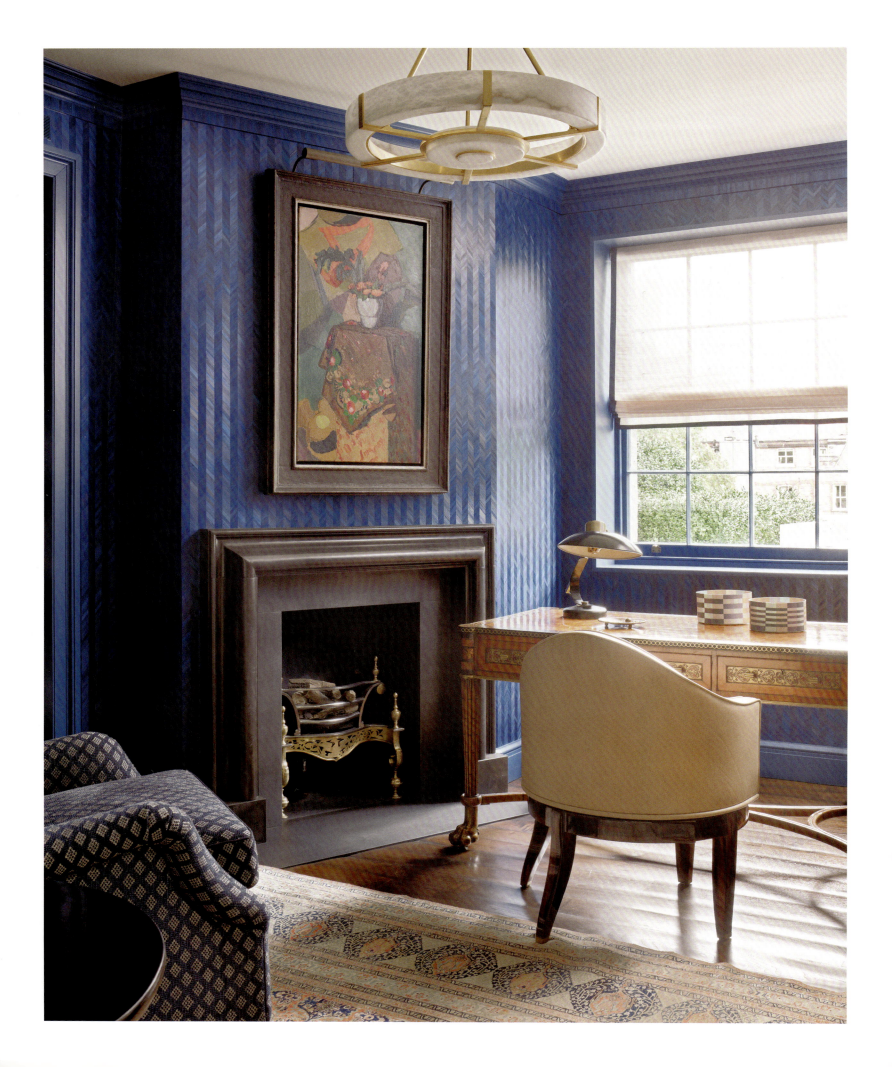

Opposite: The house's upper floors contain two studies. The gentleman's features walls paneled in dyed straw marquetry. A contemporary alabaster and brass pendant fixture floats above a deeply considered mélange of period and modern furniture. **Above:** The lady's office luxuriates in walls upholstered in a shade of pale pink peony. The translucent window blinds are embroidered with tiny pearls. The furnishings and art come together with the molded-glass chandelier in an ambience of light-infused elegance.

Preceding spread: Covered in gainaged silk velvet, the wall panels cocoon the main bedroom in an aqueous lagoon green that calls to the river beyond. A romantic custom bed sits between period end tables and lamps. Opposite: Mindfully selected, a 1930s painting depicting a light show over the Thames continues the river theme. Top: Acorns and oak leaves, one of this room's signature details, repeat in various materials and scales. Right: The whimsical gueridons seem to perform a rope trick.

Above and opposite: A small vestibule leads from the main bedroom into his-and-hers primary baths. With walls covered in a lighter shade of lagoon green linen, this area takes on its own persona. The nature of the color story establishes a visible connection between the different spaces while indicating the transition. A tented ceiling endows the vestibule with its own definitive element of decorative theater. A suspended etched-glass nineteenth-century dish chandelier adds another flourish overhead.

Opposite: In the gentleman's bathroom, a rich mélange of materials comes together to create a quiet, luxurious, masculine space. A custom vanity inspired by an antique wood sideboard combines a counter and basin of highly figured onyx atop a cast bronze base. Above left: The custom mosaic floors in both the gentleman's and lady's bath were meticulously crafted in Italy. His features two tons of marble. Above right: The closets are all behind wood frame doors inset with multiple stripes of antique leather.

Top: The glimmering mosaic floor in the lady's bath combines onyx with gold glass framed by a border of amethyst, onyx, and gold glass. Left: The closets are secreted behind *verre églomisé* doors with an overall flowering-tree pattern that harkens to the window's garden view. Opposite: Her bath is a much lighter confection in pistachio accented with purple. In a completely fanciful touch (after a discussion with the lighting designer), four crystal chandeliers provide the icing atop of the pastry.

We love residences that look, feel, and are exquisite in sense and sensibility. We design each interior as a world unto itself, a place meant to be cherished and rare for the people who live in it. While we may not fill every space with priceless things, we have a passion for what is unique, scarce, and special, as do the people whose homes we create and curate.

The classic notion of the exquisite tends to focus on lustrous metals, especially gold, platinum, and silver, as well as on gemstones such as amethyst, onyx, rock crystal, jasper, jade, malachite, lapis lazuli, and more. We relish using these elements made by the earth's remarkable alchemy to add magic to the everyday living space. And we do, in abundance: in entry doors of obsidian, rock crystal, and bronze; delicate hand-blown glass; shimmering drawer fronts and surfaces of gypsum or selenite; amethyst insets in marble floors; walls opalescing in the sheen of mother of pearl or pearlescent plaster lacquered with a metallic overlay; floors glimmering with lustrous silk and wool rugs woven with threads of gold. Even the stone slabs we select for bathroom walls, kitchen counters, islands, and tabletops are imbued with meaning because we cherish going to the stone yard to search for the perfect piece—each one is a unique natural form and a product of a distant time. We also love the more unexpected preciousness that results from transforming something ordinary, such as barn wood, into something extraordinary, with, say, a liquid metallic finish.

Luminosity, reflection, and sheen are our go-to antidotes to the flat planes that frame each interior. We love mirrors for this very reason—that they make light dance. We never shy away from mirroring a wall to establish a focal point, nor do we hesitate about mirroring an entire room. Joy comes with dreaming up new ways to manipulate reflective glass to produce something never seen before, whether it involves collaging various colors or patterns into one surface in a powder room, or insetting them into cubistic patterns to create mystery in a bar or jazz-inflected glamour in a dining room. The essential idea came to us from a photo of a French Art Deco dining room, mirrored in a typical squared grid with rosettes, by Marc Plantier. What better fun than to develop a modern riff on this traditional approach? But it is worth remembering that Plantier and his confrères, like us, also took cues from their predecessors. Every era translates the visual language of the past into an idiom that suits what is current. There is nothing new under the Sun King. This is why we so value the traditions, twists, and turns of the decorative arts and interior design, as well as the great books, libraries, museums, and houses that document them.

Perhaps most exquisite of all are the handmade components of a room, the special pieces, the intricate details, the beading, stitching, and handwork, that only take center stage when they are ready for their close-ups. The fine craftspeople whose hands fashion unique embellishments and the pieces they adorn invest whatever they do with their care, skill, and the long legacy of human invention.

EXQUISITE

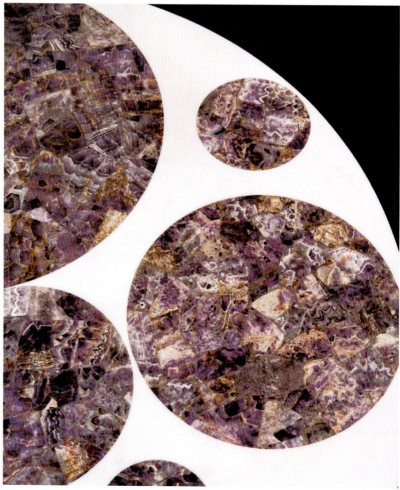

Luscious materials are one of our hallmarks as a firm. And the classic definition of hallmark—a mark stamped on articles of gold, silver, or platinum in Britain, certifying their standard of purity—aptly describes our approach. Semiprecious stones, gilt, porcelain, plaster, beading, crystal, and hand-blown glass are just some of the sublime elements we employ.

FOREVER VIEWS

For people in love with the nature of home and its infinite diversity, experiencing design's transformative powers often sparks fabulous consequences. The couple who commissioned this art-filled, craft-celebrating, full-floor aerie in Tribeca, for example, has developed a voracious appetite for upping their aesthetic game with each successive residence. The vast apartment—their fourth project with us (we finished the fifth, a glass house in upstate New York, first)—combines two three-bedroom units in a now iconic super-scraper that, at the time of purchase, existed only in blueprints. We completed our plans before a single piece of steel went in the ground. Once construction commenced, we refined our decisions with fresh eyes.

These two share a passion for food and wine, delight in hosting grand entertainments, and cherish quiet moments reading, dining, relaxing, and working side by side. To create magnets to draw them to the interior's farthest reaches, we balanced the east and west perimeters with corresponding great rooms for intimate gatherings and serious entertaining, respectively. To accommodate their wine room, gym, media lounge/guest room, kitchen, and spacious home office, we reduced the six bedrooms to four. Blocking one set of elevators (the owner's brilliant suggestion) brought clarity to the entry circulation. Throughout, materials selected for their minimalist sensibility and maximalist effect entice the couple to enjoy every last inch of their 7,300 square feet.

The duo requested uninterrupted axial views, a challenge because of fixed conditions. As often happens, the architectural givens—elevator core, slab construction, and immovable risers of various heights, beams, and columns—inspired the interior's grand gestures. We submerged low-rise elements within lakelike lacquered wood platforms and plinths, and clad the forest of risers and columns in tantalizing metallized plaster. To marry divergent ceiling heights, we dropped a series of lima bean-shaped panels; swooping soffits amplify the path of the eye to the views. Like proud sequoias, a trio of interior columns with dimensional finish details inspired by Asian ink paintings and the work of Arnaldo Pomodoro earthily command the east great room. In the airy west great room, the fireplace focuses the different seating groups and an expansive dining area capitalizes on the city's theatrical sunsets. The kitchen is all rich, dark surfaces. In shades from aqua to coppery peach, the primary bedroom is all textured radiance.

The furnishings—those of our design and those by today's great makers—together with the wide ranging art and intricate filigree of detail elevate this couple's gravity-defying vision to its bold yet nuanced culmination. Thrilling for them, and for us, too.

Page 80: An anthropomorphic bench by the Haas Brothers is emblematic of the sense of wit that pervades an otherwise serene apartment. **Preceding spread:** In the west great room, an intimate seating area by the fireplace instills coziness with style. The shapely cocktail table inserts another note of whimsy. **Above:** A lounge chair in gold helps to warm the room's cool urban grays. An asymmetrically positioned ceramic art installation creates unique rhythm on the fireplace wall. **Opposite:** The entry into the west great room is lined in bronze and wood. Playful paintings beside the entry, strongly anchored by sculptural bronze benches, harken to the flying chandelier beyond.

Preceding spread: The dining room takes pride of place with a custom table of ebonized mahogany and gold leaf that can seat as many as eighteen. **Top:** The chandelier's gold leaf–lined shades glow warmly when lit. **Right:** Hand-carved and gilded, the concave ends of the table base radiate a subtle glimmer that relates to the gold leather strips in the chairs' hand-woven upholstery. **Opposite:** The columns are slathered in metallic plaster to celebrate their monumental structure. The sculpture is by Tony Cragg.

Opposite: In the open kitchen, the tonal and materials palette takes a bold graphic stance. The sculptural island makes a strong statement as it embraces one of the building's structural columns. The honed marble and quartzite elements combine in architectural harmony to establish work and dining surfaces. **Above:** The cabinetry is in ebonized wood, which richly sets off the patinated steel hood. With a curved end for comfort, the peninsula is sufficiently substantial to accommodate back-to-back sinks.

Above: Scaled for intimacy, the handcrafted table of maple and marble by John Eric Byers compels the touch. **Opposite:** Just beyond the peninsula, a nook arranged for two takes full advantage of the spectacular view. The intimate space includes a pair of very comfortable custom armchairs on either side of a table that perfectly suits a shared conversation over a continental breakfast enjoyed with a leisurely coffee. For just that reason, the coffee maker is conveniently integrated into the adjacent bar.

Preceding spread: One of this residence's numerous bedrooms transitioned into an intimate media room over the course of the reconfiguration. The deep sofa can do double duty as a bed when the occasion calls. The leather panels that surround the TV on the opposite wall add dimensional interest. The room's several nods to nature include the multilevel low table that incorporates hunks of ebonized wood and a pair of table lamps with sweeping bases that resemble tree trunks. **Above:** The subtlest of satin welts that details the velvet upholstery matches the bolsters. **Opposite:** In close-up, the low table by Stefan Bishop shows the compelling beauty of the natural wood grain.

Opposite: In the large home office, an important part of the program, a partners' desk of our design seats the couple side-by-side so they can both enjoy the view. Barbara Takenaga's polyptych seems to embody the cityscape beyond. The custom cabinet behind the desk incorporates a mirrored back specifically to display the owners' collection of antique cameras from all sides. Above: A pair of lounge chairs with a shared ottoman rests right next to the window, an inviting spot for quiet contemplation.

Above: The main bedroom suite incorporates dual dressing rooms. Hers has closets obscured behind specialty glass. A spiritual crystal dangles from the lantern. **Left:** The dresser puts a toothy smile on the face of all who see it. The rug resembles a map of lower Manhattan as seen through the windows. **Opposite:** Iridescent horsehair wall covering swathes the bedroom in an aurora of apricot and palest aqua. The custom bed with gainage headboard and footboard is a contemporary take on an antique technique.

Opposite: Necessity is so often the mother of design invention, as in the dramatic solution for the east great room's challenging conditions. Clad in bronze-finished cylinders, immovable mechanical columns create massive "trees." These ascend out of lacquered "lakes," which conceal more immovables, and soar into gently curved ceiling soffits that tie together the residence's east and west ends. **Above:** A gilded metal sculpture echoes the surrounding forms. **Following spread:** The sensuous furniture forms reiterate recurring motifs. On the back wall, a gray stone inset and counter incorporate a wet bar. In the corner, a table—another tree form—invites intimate dining.

Above: At the other end of the east great room, a chaise by Vladimir Kagan enjoys two mesmerizing views: the fireplace and the cityscape. Opposite: This seating group, one of three in the room, convenes around the fireplace. Following spread: A plush rug defines boundaries of this seating group, which nests organically into a well-windowed corner. Walls gain texture with a Venetian plaster treatment. A custom metallic finish transforms the corner's large mechanical column into a sculptural presence.

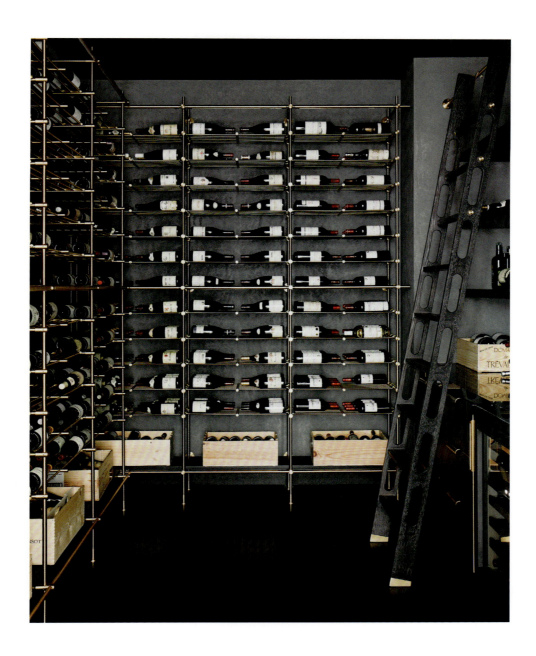

Opposite: In the lady's bathroom, expanses of luminous honey-colored onyx and the palest cerused oak come together with back-painted glass, mirror, and polished nickel details to create a harmonious retreat of the quietest luxury. **Above:** The climate-controlled wine cellar amply memorializes the client's true passion for the grape. Walls finished in waterproof Venetian plaster are home to a custom floor-to-ceiling storage system of purpose-built shelving constructed of oak and satin and polished brass.

CALEB'S APARTMENT

New York has the kind of architectural history that Texas lacks, which is probably why I love the city's prewar apartment buildings and the glamorous rooms I envision behind their facades. This apartment, for example, had been in the same family since the 1920s, when the building first opened. It was a time capsule when I purchased it. I liked the proper rooms. I knew that the way the spaces unfolded would allow me to create isolated yet connected moments and experiences. The one real architectural revision I made involved reconfiguring a small maid's room next to the kitchen to create the main bathroom, now a marble-lined wet room. Of course, I enhanced the plaster moldings and details and added elegant millwork, all to make the classic modish.

As happy as traditional interiors make me, I need the contemporary insertions. I delight in the mix. The contrast of modern and old? Rooms that each speak to the seasons, moods, and emotions, but still relate to one another? These instincts form the double helix of my design DNA. I am one to establish tone and character at the front door, carry it—and vary it—through to the bedroom.

Here, the conversation starts in the foyer with contemporary lacquer panels—Jamie's suggestion, instead of classic moldings—providing a sleek backdrop to nineteenth-, twentieth-, and twenty-first-century pieces, including some of my design. Singly and together, these components hint subtly at the textures, forms, and materials to come. The living room, serene and calming with touches of the foyer's neutral hue, introduces flashes of stronger colors that offer clues to the bolder rooms ahead. The library, where I spend most of my time, feels like being in the park; the daybed, so comfortable for lounging, has an upholstered mattress that allows the room to do double duty for guests. The kitchen explores my concept of a black, but not all-black, workspace. The dining room, hot in hue, walks the formal/casual line with walls mirrored in a Mondrian rhythm and a lacquered ceiling. The bedroom hallway feels like a dark cave with the pull of art at the end, thanks to an installation by Christina Watka. The bedroom itself, swathed in deepest midnight blue for sleeping, luxuriates in the textural dance of marble, moiré, and velvet.

The different forms of rock crystal, which I love, add in touches of nature's wonder here and there throughout. Taken individually and all together, these rooms reflect and express the different facets of me.

Page 112: The foyer sets up the contrast of traditional and contemporary styles. Previous spread: The living room is serene yet makes a statement with its overall lightness. The punctuating colors of the pillows and art hint at the more saturated rooms to come. Opposite: Fluting and rock crystal are recurring motifs. Top: The classical early-twentieth-century Italian vase balances the triptych by Vicky Barranguet. Right: The crystal side table offsets the nineteenth-century chair's fancier language.

Above: The stacked fireplace mirror by Sam Baron creates an optical illusion, changing forms and shifting dimensions from different angles; it also plays into the fluting on the fireplace wall. The nineteenth-century sconces with crystal drops add interesting contrast. Opposite: The sensuous forms of Vladimir Kagan's chairs and ottoman embody the sweeping gestures that are one of this room's defining design elements. Ann Aspinwall's artworks by the fireplace insert controlled moments of vibrant color.

Opposite: The sofa, one of my designs, was not only made for this space but constructed on the premises because of its size; its channel-tufted back and the columnar curtain panels vary the fluted detail. **Above:** In this somewhat muted room, the touches of golden brass and gilt reflect light beautifully. The interlocking curves of the hammered-brass cocktail tables, another of my site-specific designs, take cues from the triptych's painterly swoops, as do the Roman shades and many of the textiles. The rug's slight change in pile height also emulates these curves very subtly. Porcelain and flowers, two loves, come together in the blooms by Matthew Solomon.

Top: The library, a multifunctional room, captures and reflects light in a very energizing way. Left: The flame-stitch fabric pulls in nuances of the palette and relates closely to the wall covering from Alpha Workshops. Opposite: The daybed, an upholstered mattress, is perfect for lounging and TV watching, and can double as a bed when necessary. The wall covering has a metallic mylar background, so there really is a glow. The painting, by Allison Gildersleeve, resembles a dreamy walk through nature.

Opposite: The addition of moldings and pilasters, which wrap around the room to create the bookcases, give the room structure and symmetry. A nineteenth-century bureau plat, purchased at auction, helps satisfy a love of antiques. The ceiling fixture is reminiscent of the sun, and just as joyful. The cashmere rug feels luxurious underfoot. Above left: With an attached full bath, the room converts easily into an inviting guest suite. Above right: The orbs are part of my rock crystal collection.

Top: The Japanese painted bowl ties into the palette. Left: The 1970s sconces reflect glowingly off the walls. Opposite: The dining room may be small, but it is all drama, and just as fun for a dinner party as a poker game. The mirror treatment, inspired by the bar in our Kips Bay 2018 salon, has a Mondrian-like pattern. The custom dining table is made from a slab of Golden Spider marble. The 1920s Baccarat chandelier twinkles above the Tommi Parzinger candelabras. The chairs are by Milo Baughman.

Opposite: This is a wonderful room to cook in when time permits, especially with the view past the stove. A little garden grows to the left; to the right, a series of plates hand-painted with abstract faces animates the wall. The mobile might be impractical, but it inserts such a playful note. **Above:** Initially planned as a variation on a black-and-white kitchen, it ultimately skewed darker. With more black than white, and red accents in the glass mosaic floors, it ties into the adjoining dining room.

Above: The door handles, one of our firm's designs for SA Baxter, incorporate the flute motif in another form. **Opposite:** A ceramic installation by Christine Watka transforms one wall of the main bedroom into a celestial fantasy or an archipelago with a purposeful scattering of individually crafted pieces, some gilded. **Following spread:** The main bedroom is a cocoon wrapped in deepest, darkest moiré brightened by sparkling notes of gold and crystal, luminous shagreen, and a few bolts of turquoise. Behind the bed, a series of velvet-upholstered panels creates a rich backdrop for a painting by Matthias Meyer. A luxuriously plush shearling rug is a treat for bare feet.

Opposite: The slabs of figured marble that line the floor and walls of the bathroom in an ombré of aqueous shades of blue seem to materialize the many moods of water. A 1960s glass ceiling fixture interjects something of a floral note overhead. Top left: The natural striations of the marble also relate very directly to the tones and ripples of the bedroom's moiré-covered walls. Top right: The contemporary sconces pick up on the orb motif that repeats through the apartment in various scales and materials.

Our hallmark is a dynamic eclecticism, a bold yet finely calibrated balance between timelessness and today. We are confident in our view of how to bring disparate elements together to radiate a distinctive allure and tell a uniquely expressive story. The foundation of this sense of conviction rests in the decision-making behind the design. The two of us cannot help but have our respective takes on glamour, curation, and elegance. Yet we share an eye for the definite, edited, and concise. Our agreement on where the line of beauty lies, on how far to push and when to stop, allows us to take visual risks while maintaining the desired level of sophistication and elegance.

The ever-evolving lexicon of styles provides us with a broad set of parameters, a barometer of choice, as it were. We delight in the challenge of the singular mix, in creating visual, physical, and emotional comfort with components from various periods, cultures, and eras that seem to have no preordained relationships. We love it when a serious antique, perhaps a marvelous pair of inimitable, wonderfully odd nineteenth-century chairs with a fabulous patina, sidles up to something with a brash, obviously contemporary personality, say a commanding piece of furniture or lighting by one of today's artisans that may be a bit provocative. On their own, the individual designs are memorable. Together, their visual chemistry makes an original statement. The contrast proves to be the catalyst, and the enchantress.

The architectural shell serves as the canvas on which we build compositions of line, form, color, texture, pattern, and materials. The silhouette of a curved sofa, for example, may inspire us to introduce a strong, linear gesture; punctuated with pillows in gorgeous colors that appear in another tone on a curtain; that sofa functions as far more than its essential geometry, or merely a seat. A forceful ceiling detail, a line of molding that opens as it rises like an opera aria gives heightened expression to space; the cove lighting provides an accenting crescendo, further highlighting the shape and line. The details can be subtle. They can be bold. But they come together to create unique, powerful spaces for our clients.

Repetition conveys confidence. Reprising a particular facet of a room—whether color, form, or texture—establishes a rhythm that defines the space and simultaneously communicates self-assurance. Envision a nineteenth-century apartment with its original millwork details illuminated literally and metaphorically by a series of bold, angular, faceted, and over-scaled lanterns marching staunchly overhead down the entry hall with an audaciously contemporary carpet underfoot. In our salon in the Kips Bay Show House of 2018, we deployed circular forms in all their variety, with unexpected divergences in period, creating an immediately apparent effect that, once absorbed, proved a subtle reminder of an assertive decision.

We care most about what lives best together. What material combinations feel interesting. What forms show off the others to greatest advantage. What colors, patterns, and textures provide the necessary levels of harmony and dissonance to keep the vision compelling. With every interior, the moment arrives when we know we need to add a discordant note in the scheme to generate additional visual excitement, tension, and that extra oomph—an element that talks to the other pieces around it, makes us smile, and intrigues us enough to look more closely, to savor, and remember.

CONFIDENT

When the gestures of design are large and sweeping, BOLD is the natural result. Every decision we make, we do so with confidence—to the finest detail. The juxtaposition of eclectic furnishings, art, and accessories from varied centuries and cultures, as well as the insertion of provocative eye candy placed just so, are among the tools we use to delight the eye.

GEORGIAN REMIX

At their finest, destiny and design operate hand in hand. When these clients happened upon this glorious neo-Georgian brick classic designed by F. Burrall Hoffman, architect of Miami's famed Vizcaya, it was a case of dream house by serendipity. The house's architectural challenges were legion, as it had had no significant structural or mechanical upgrades since 1910. The charge was to maintain the essence of the original even as we reconfigured major aspects, replaced ungainly earlier additions, and introduced new structures, including a pool house, outbuildings, and barns, honoring the original architecture while making clear that the Long Island property is now absorbed in the present tense.

In their deepest souls, these clients love the antique, especially the eighteenth and nineteenth centuries. They also enthusiastically embrace the now and the unfamiliar to their eyes. The dialectic of their wide-ranging interests in design, art, and artifact begins in the foyer, which exemplifies the spirit of our approach. Here, the floor and stair rail are original, albeit meticulously restored; the plasterwork details are our refinements. So, too, are the marble stairs, facsimiles of the original painted wood and much more in keeping with the entry's classicism. Within this framework, a bronze piano, Alexander Calder mobile, dominating Roy Lichtenstein painting, and contemporary consoles surmounted by antique mirrors and sconces make the case for bold contrast. The dining room does the same with its new millwork wainscoting (our updated take on the classic linen fold), as well as a Maya Lin wall sculpture and chandelier on a hydraulic lift, both commissions.

The full eclecticism of our aesthetic journey comes to the fore in the living room. Taking center stage, a Vladimir Kagan tête-à-tête cozies up to 1940s French chairs, nineteenth-century consoles, and Tang Dynasty horses. Seating arrangements at each end embrace the heady mix with English Hepplewhite chairs, contemporary cocktail tables and consoles mingling with 1940s Jansen sofas and lounge chairs.

One hundred years in, the oak-panels of the library not only needed replacing, but the built-in shelves were too shallow for a library of art books. Recreated in mahogany with deep, parchment-lined bookcases, this room now exemplifies space as lustrous embrace. In the sunroom, the clients' interest in the different inspired the choice of marvelous, idiosyncratic suspended steel hammocks.

The main bedroom, a confection in orchid and melon, is our response to the clients' favorite combination of purple and orange. The lady's and gentleman's baths make equally bold statements, with custom marble flooring in his-and-hers colorations that nod to the past with twenty-first-century panache.

When the desired aesthetic champions an eclectic design dialectic, fortune favors the bold.

Page 142: A newly created envelope with classical architectural elements based on the period originals, the foyer of this 1910 house celebrates surprising juxtapositions of antique, vintage, modern, and contemporary elements. **Top:** A marble stair reinterprets its painted-wood predecessor and supports the restored original railing. **Above:** The tale of contrasts complexifies. **Right:** The eclectic mix previews the rooms to come.

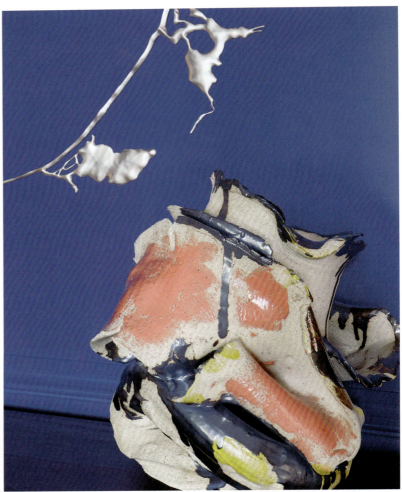

Preceding spread: The dining room's furnishings, primarily traditional in nature, meld confidently with contemporary elements, including the art and the chandelier. Swathed in a vibrant lacquer finish, the paneled envelope incorporates an updated take on a classic linenfold detail, which gives the wainscot its distinctive presence. **Above left:** Sinuous candelabras play to the surroundings. **Above right:** An installation commissioned from Maya Lin dances delicately across one wall partnered, for a turn, by a hefty contemporary ceramic. **Opposite:** Crystal chandeliers designed for the room echo the wainscot's linenfold fluting and raise and lower as the occasion requires.

Preceding spread: The living room is an elemental statement of our love of eclecticism. A 1970s roundabout centers the expansive space. Other furnishings range from French 1940s chairs to English nineteenth-century consoles and ancient Chinese horses. The contemporary painting is a marvelous contrast to the original antique mantel. **Above:** These clients delightedly embrace the unexpected. **Opposite:** The primary coral color warms the space with accents of blue and surprising shots of egg yolk.

Preceding spread: The design of this classical mahogany library incorporates inset parchment-wrapped bookshelves, a contemporary insertion intended to add a lightness to the room. Balancing these are embroidered off-white curtains and the wheat-colored carpet. The furnishings are dressed in shades of red for conviviality and warmth. **Opposite:** The mix seen throughout the house continues. **Top and right:** The selections prioritize artistry and craft and range from the Art Deco to the purely today.

Above: Adjacent to the living room, the sunroom takes the egg yolk accents and uses them full throttle. Right: The client requested a change from conventional seating, so two steel hammocks that hang from the ceiling offer unique places for contemplation.

Opposite: The renovation blew out multiple original rooms of the 1910 house to create the capacious kitchen and breakfast area. At 27 feet in length, the center island is a true tour de force that combines the darkest espresso walnut and chiseled oak with a gray cerused finish. **Above:** The purple flecked terrazzo floor, which climbs up to top the island, connects to the purple accents that wind their way into the backsplash, cabinet fronts, and chair upholstery. A live-edge table beckons invitingly.

Top left: A modern coffee table adds a delightful element of wit to the intimate salon just off the kitchen. **Top right:** A mid-century modern candelabrum plays to the room's antecedents. **Opposite:** The elegant pale wood paneling that wraps the salon makes a very oblique reference to the suburban rec rooms of the 1950s. Leather and velvet furnishings provide assertive accents that also tie into the large photo collage by Vik Muniz of George Washington crossing the Delaware above a whimsical 1960s lamp.

Opposite: Her bathroom with a patterned marble floor opens directly onto her ravishing dressing room. **Above:** The main bedroom suite is aglow in the sunrise/sunset tones of orchid and melon, an interpretation of the client's favorite color combination of purple and orange. The sleeping chamber features custom embroidered curtains and accessories in these roseate hues. **Following spread:** This tangelo painted retreat, one of the house's many guest rooms, is a delightful nest for any overnight visitor.

Opposite: Extensive gardens surround the house in a layered landscape. One area of the welcoming upper terrace centers on a bronze fire pit that leads the eye directly to a totemic Tony Cragg sculpture, right at home amid the surrounding towering trees, and then into the restored rose garden beyond. **Above:** In a garden green room adjacent to the pool, a magnificent terra-cotta urn raised majestically on a stone plinth marks the point where the various pathways to different outdoor destinations meet.

Opposite: Layer upon layer of lush plantings devised by Janice Parker Landscape Architects frame the pool terrace. Above: A nineteenth-century sculpture of Amphitrite, the goddess of the sea and Poseidon's wife, presides over her aqueous domain.

Above: The terrace immediately adjacent to the rear of the house is a gracious exterior living space furnished comfortably for conversation and lounging. **Opposite:** Refreshed and restored to its classical glory, this symmetrical, perfectly proportioned Georgian house from 1910 proudly wears its red brick cladding with appropriately crisp white trim and dark green shutters. Immediately to the right of the front door, an enormous antique clock face connotes time's passage—and the house's timeless beauty.

AN IDEAL
AERIE

For those who cherish Saul Steinberg's iconic vision of Manhattan from 20,000 feet up across the grid and over the river to the great beyond, there is nothing quite like a sprawling pied-à-ciel in one of the storied super scrapers on Billionaires' Row. This international family, long desirous of a permanent New York base for their frequent visits Stateside, found just such an ethereal perch, with panoramic views of the city skyline, Central Park, and all points north.

The wife happened to be an aficionado of the finest contemporary design and modern art, which set our aesthetic direction. While the two of them wished to live in a unique world furnished with objects of great beauty, they naturally desired that the views take center stage. We devised a background palette of platinum and pearl, with accents of cobalt, wisteria, lavender, and citrine, to animate the spaces, quietly. Within, a potpourri of materials—wood, lacquer, stone, gypsum, glass, velvet, leather, mirror, and bronze—mix and mingle provocatively and evocatively throughout. We also commissioned and collected pieces from today's great makers and assembled an arresting array of artworks—by Elaine de Kooning, Barbara Takenaga, Tony Cragg, Rob Wynne, and Matthew Solomon, among others—to imbue the airy spaces with the requisite expressive character, personality, and drama.

First, though, the new construction required perfecting and refinement. To better focus the views, we adjusted the proportions of the openings between the spaces. We also upgraded all the lighting, HVAC grills, and covers, and refinished all the walls with hefty, luxurious materials from plaster to velvet for strength and superb quality.

The couple wanted to celebrate the uninterrupted flow between the living room and dining room along a 60-foot expanse overlooking Central Park and the northern boroughs, while still shielding the sight lines between the two spaces for when they entertain. We accomplished this by introducing a floating wall clad in verre églomisé, a glamorous gesture that conceals the TV.

In the living area, two seating groups provide amply for large and intimate gatherings. The dining room, quite formal, centers on a long, lacquered table on top of a glimmering, woven-metal floor covering. In every space, carefully considered pieces subtly—or not—layer distinctive points of interest into the surroundings. The main bedroom, a silk-velvet wrapped cocoon tinged in touches of wisteria, practically merges into the cloud line. Such is the joy of living on cloud nine.

Page 174: Dramatic black and gold furnishings and celestial art announce the entry to this dreamy apartment in the clouds. **Left:** Elegantly fluted plaster envelops the foyer, endowing it with solidity. **Top and above:** The cloakroom and adjacent powder room are lined in gold leaf and mother-of-pearl-finished panels created by artist Nancy Lorenz.

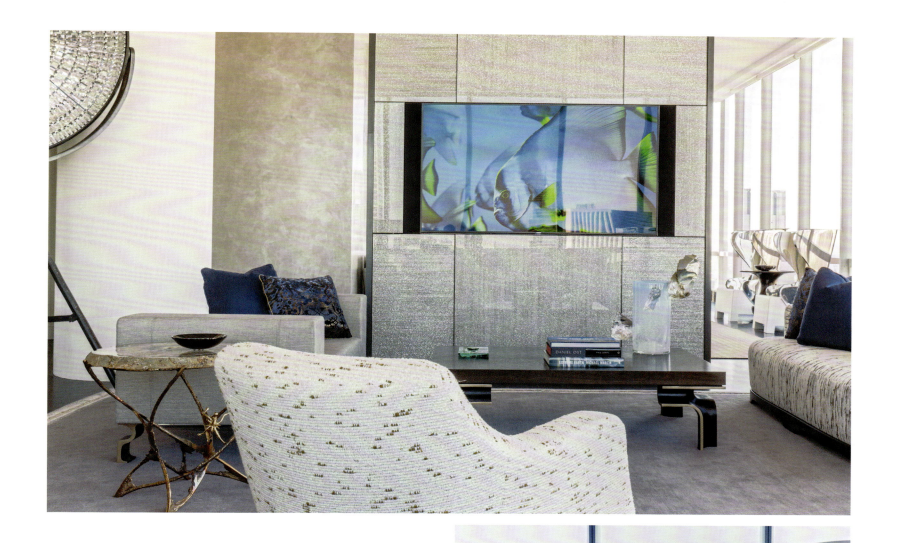

Preceding spread: The serene living room maintains the bold point of view established in the foyer. Two seating groups are as welcoming for private reflection and intimate tête-à-têtes as for larger gatherings. **Opposite, above, right:** Contemporary pieces by modern artisans furnish the space. A floating wall of chiseled and silvered glass magically conceals the TV. Voluptuous textures cover the upholstered pieces. **Following spread:** The second seating group purposefully takes in the skyline view.

Above: The aerie's airy dining room centers on a glistening white table surrounded by elegant chairs dressed in woven leather and satin. All sit lightly atop a woven rug, a custom commission. Opposite: The chandelier floats elegantly overhead, its orbs rather like cumulus clouds that may have wafted in through the windows. A fanciful, floral ceramic garniture commissioned from the late ceramicist Matthew Solomon marches down the center of the table, an allusion to rootedness and the earth far below.

Top: A syncopated painting infuses vibrant color into the kitchen. **Above:** A galactic glass asteroid of a chandelier invigorates the space. **Right:** Dark macassar cabinetry and granite countertops contrast graphically with the whiteness of the public rooms.

Preceding spread: With fully upholstered walls and swaths of hand-painted curtains, the serene main bedroom is richly cocooned in silk velvet, which seductively captures and reflects the changing light. Opposite: The heady mix of materials continues with lacquer, selenite, metallic leather, porcelain, marble, and glass. A plush rug grounds the room on a surface of ethereal pattern that connects to the sky and the skyline beyond. Above: The balance of forms and textures compels the eye and the touch.

There are few satisfactions in life as wonderful as making someone smile. If we can accomplish this using the elements at our disposal—the tools and tricks of the interior designer's trade—what could be better? This is where wit, visual wit, enters the design scenario.

We feel each home should be the most perfect possible expression of its owner's personality, created from the most perfect possible components, and perfectly unique in mood and atmosphere. Too much perfection, though, tends to get in the way of the livability and pleasure that are always our aim. Every room, no matter how ravishing or glamorous, benefits from the inclusion of at least one element that generates a double take, lightens the room's spirit, or knocks out a bit of the proverbial wind: that stroke of visual humor, that adjacency or relationship that delights with surprise because it invigorates everything around it.

Imagine a cocoon of a primary bedroom, shimmering with luscious, luxe, iridescent materials visible and touchable from every vantage point. It would certainly be dreamy beyond words. But incorporate a dresser with some sexy curves, yet that resembles a molar—a piece superbly functional, yet quietly funny—and voilá. Or envision a white-clad living room, graced with pieces by some of the world's finest contemporary makers, overlooking cinematic urban vistas. It would make absolute design sense to place a lamp of enormous proportions in one corner to balance the exposed structural columns. But opt for a veritable klieg light of industrial steel and Swarovski crystals, and the room is camera-ready for its close-up.

Visual wit, like the best of humor, offers the element of intellectual engagement; of provocation. It prods us not only to think, but also to examine our preconceptions and find delight in the process of coming to terms with them. Some of today's great makers specialize in doing precisely this, using their legerdemain to render the facetious and clever in the most elegant way, or basing an entire body of work on what is droll, and on spearing our preconceived notions of appropriateness. So often, these kinds of pieces reflect what our clients find amusing, which is why we so love collaborating with these talents on one-of-a-kind pieces for specific interiors.

Whenever we commission a piece, we carefully consider the strengths of the artist or artisan, and work with those strengths to conceive and make something truly exceptional and original for the specific space, client, and spot. Our point of departure is often something the artisan has already brought into being, which we then alter by scale, color, or material. To add a flourish to a dining room floating high in the urban sky, for example, we asked one great ceramicist to create a garniture de table. Brilliantly, through his artist's vision, he prestidigitated an assemblage of tulips, other flowers, and roots into a remarkable porcelain garden that left the planet earth and came to rest aloft.

Interiors are at their best, we believe, when they transcend the merely comfortable, easy, and pretty. Visual wit—the magical element of just the right, curated surprise—provides a point of conversation, a fizz of effervescence, an antidote to the harshness of everyday life. It serves as the exclamation point, or occasionally the question mark, that elicits the grin we cherish, while bringing everything around it into sharper focus.

W I T T Y

Creating residences of beauty and delight, ones that truly fulfill a client's program, is our main goal. Yet, we think this should be done with joy. To this end, adding touches of wit is one of our favorite devices. Anthropomorphic forms crawling and rising from tabletops, fantastic little beasts, a contemporary take on tulipomania—all are sly smile inducers.

THE LIGHT FANTASTIC

In the hunt for living space, New Yorkers tend to honor the urban dweller's first commandment: Let there be light! If the place comes with views, too, well, fabulous! This family with two teenagers followed that directive when they opted out of their longtime Tribeca maisonette and into this airy apartment that sails like a cruise ship above the Hudson River. Because the building was under construction at the time of purchase, we were able to perfectly tailor the planned six-bedroom, eight-bath residence with an 80-foot, wrap-around terrace for the family's lifestyle. Specifically, we reconfigured one bedroom and bath into a study with a media area and wet bar. We also created a capacious playroom with a basketball court and a second media area.

We began establishing the light, playful attitude they desired in the intimate foyer. Here, a shades-of-white palette is differentiated by a textural mix—dimensional plaster walls (its circular motif cycles throughout), parchment-wrapped console, and eggshell-inlay mirror frame—and focused by ebonized and satin brass accents. The space brightens further in the contiguous living and dining areas (all expansive under higher ceilings), which flow into the kitchen and breakfast area, as well as out to the terrace. In the living room, we deployed a back-to-back biscuit-tufted sofa (in a very durable white fabric) to define two seating areas atop a vast oval rug strewn with stylized lily pads in grades of blue, a nod to the nautical.

This family loves to entertain, so when we designed the table for the dining area—its extremely durable resin top recalls swirling eddies—we also devised a furniture plan for occasions requiring multiple tables. Overhead, we added a chandelier that suggests the flow of water, with bubbles of handblown glass and tendrils of delicate brass chain; for storage and service capacity, we slipped in a long buffet lacquered the darkest midnight blue. The kitchen and breakfast area palette we spiked with joyous notes of Schiaparelli pink for contrast. In the library, which doubles as the husband's home office and a den with a wet bar, we went dark, framing pickled oak millwork and stained walnut and leather furnishings with a jewel-toned stained abaca wall covering.

To instill a sexy vibe in the ethereal main bedchamber, we opted for a textural play of plush fabrics, leather, lacquer, alabaster, and brass. We could not help but extend the romance into the adjacent sitting room with a crème fraîche palette heightened by a few touches of blush pink as soft as the softest kiss.

Let there be light!

Page 198: For light-craving clients, the foyer sets the tone with hand-applied plaster walls, parchment-wrapped cabinet doors, and an eggshell-lacquered mirror. **Preceeding spread:** The well-windowed great room explodes with brightness. A custom oval rug anchors the living area on a bed of "lily pads". **Top:** Tufted seating adds to the textural play. **Left:** The rug incorporates multiple materials for tactile richness; the various blues recall the river outside. **Opposite:** The dining area inverts the color scheme.

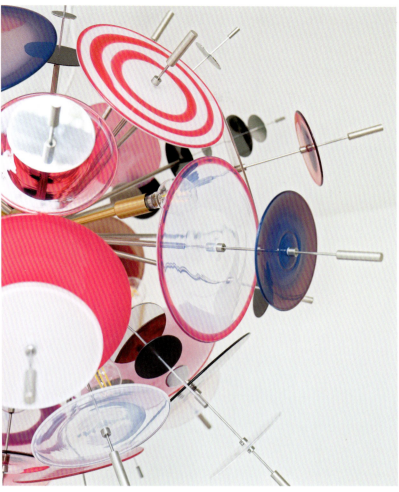

Opposite: The pop of pink accents and bubble pendants amp up the kitchen's given blonde wood cabinets and a sleek stone island. **Above left:** Large dollops of shocking pink in the banquette upholstery, the welting of the chairs and counter stools, and the asteroid of the area's chandelier overhead joyfully invigorate the predominantly neutral tones of the kitchen and the essentially white space of the adjacent breakfast area. **Above right:** The playful, colorful chandelier is the owner's favorite piece.

Top and right: The library provides the exception that reinforces the rule of this residence's lightness of being. From pale and muted at the floor to deep and saturated on the walls and furnishings, a rich ombre of luscious greens envelops this space. The natural striations of the hand-woven wall covering reappear in the hardware details and in the stone surfaces of the built-in wet bar. **Opposite:** Designed and outfitted for multiple functions, the library serves as both a home office and a media room.

Opposite: The main bedroom suite is a creamy, dreamy confection. **Top:** A desk for the lady of the house fits neatly into a window bay. The darker hem of the curtain panels lends a touch of gravity. **Right:** Palest powder pink accents whisper among the primary shades of off-white and ivory.

Above: A long, rather narrow terrace is truly furnished for everyday outdoor living. The space is expansive enough to accommodate three separate, quite substantial groupings. A large, comfortable seating area graciously extends the perimeter of the living room into the riverside landscape, so to speak. Conveniently just adjacent, though not shown, is a ping pong table that easily converts for dining. **Opposite:** At the terrace's far end, the main bedroom suite unfolds to an intimate, sheltered retreat.

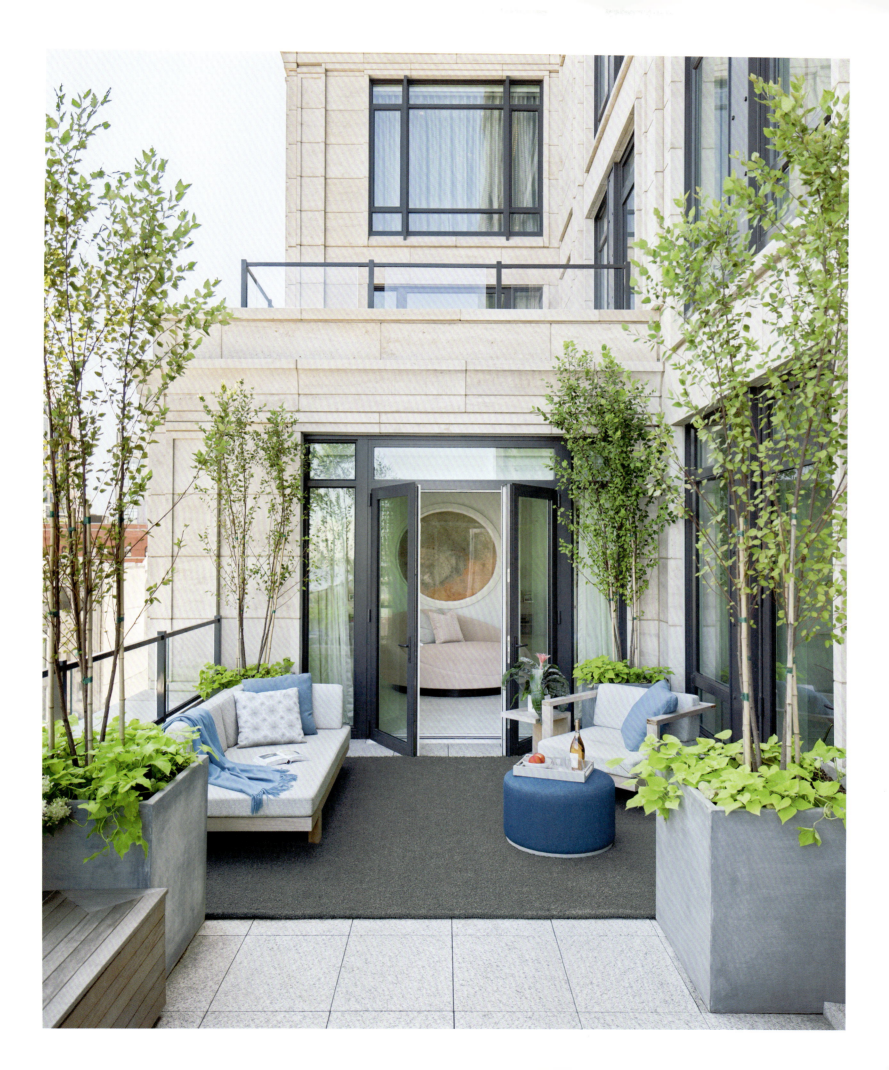

DESERT PARADISE

Everyone we work with has their own dream of domestic paradise. For these longtime clients based in the upper Midwest, Paradise Valley, Arizona, has always been both second home and nirvana in the sun. Once their grown children embarked on families of their own, the couple decided the time had come to upgrade to a larger, much more beautiful property that could accommodate all the generations together. The two envisioned generous spaces bathed in the crystalline light of their treasured Western landscape; arranged with the ease and flow of an open plan; designed and smartly furnished for casual, elegant modern living; and seamlessly connected to exterior spaces outfitted for all sorts of activities, with a casita for visiting family and guests.

We worked as the impresario with their chosen architect to bring these ideas from blueprint to built reality. The ground floor features a vast great room that unfolds into the bar, dining area, and kitchen, all with options for gathering, as well as the primary bedroom suite with a fireplace, her home office, and a his-and-hers bath limned in luminous alabaster. Upstairs, a balcony overlooking the great room attaches to guest rooms and his home office, which doubles as another bedroom when needed. The casita encompasses a guest room and en-suite bath, a bunk room, media room, gym, and pool bath.

We began by touring stone yards. These two surprised us with their passion for very chromatic, dramatic stones, which took on a starring role as we developed the various layers of materials, textures, and furnishings. The interior's color story—cactus greens and pale blue-y gray greens, with accents of Indian Paintbrush red—derives from the dramatic stone fireplace wall and from the desert's rich, varied palette. From the porcelain floor pavers to the upholstery fabrics, we deployed these hues throughout in varying degrees of intensity and saturation. The materials palette is equally evocative: an amalgam of leather, suede, and lacquer alongside a mix of metals, glass, and fabrics in luxurious textures and sheens. Because this couple had so appreciated the art collection we assembled for their corporate headquarters, they enthusiastically charged us to find wonderful, bold, large-scale works, abstract and figurative, to add impact to these capacious spaces. The result is their own delightful desert wonderland, a new place in the sun for making more family memories.

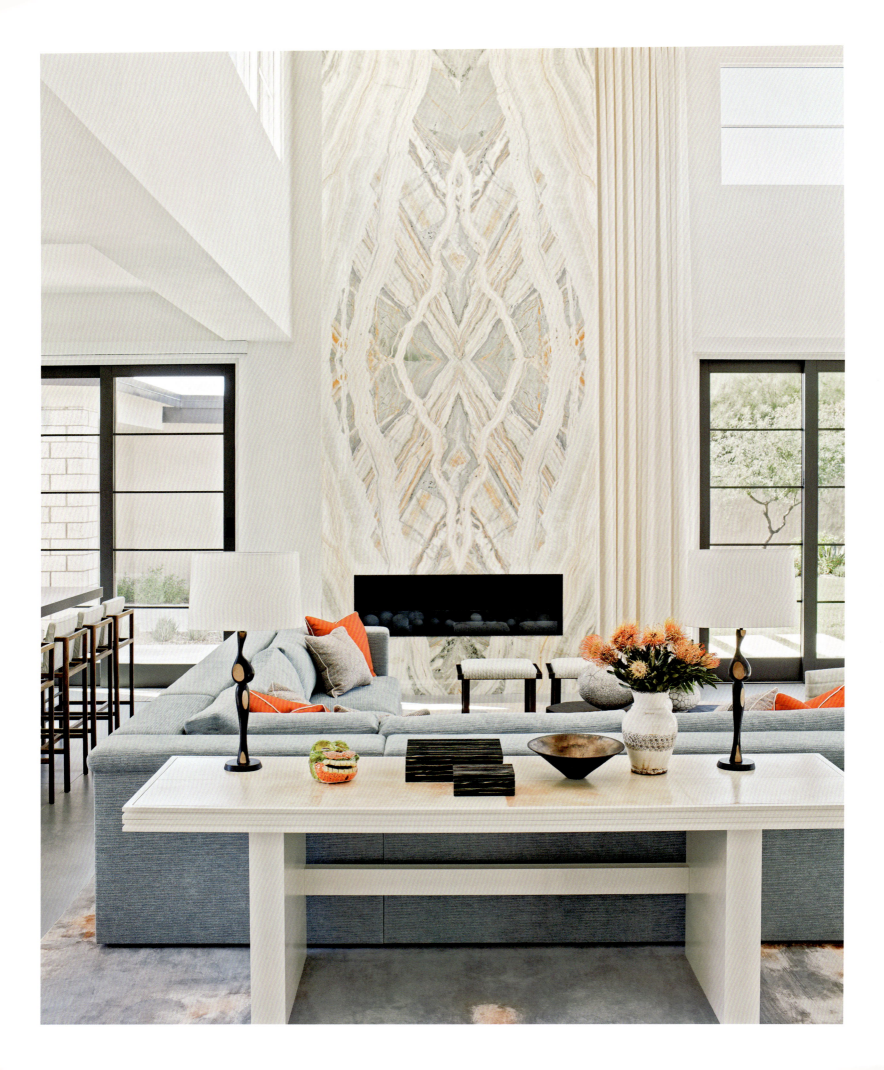

Page 212: This dream second home maximizes seamless transitions between the interior and exterior living spaces. **Preceding spread:** The heart of the house is a cavernous volumetric great room designed with an open plan for contemporary living. **Opposite:** The intimate main seating area centers on a dramatic stone-clad fireplace. The year-round arrangement includes an adjacent bar. **Above:** The color palette pulls in a harmonious array of pale, neutral, and bold hues from the surrounding desert landscape.

Preceding spread: A monumental painting by Dan Christensen anchors the dining area, a virtual glass-framed pavilion that extends organically into furnished exterior rooms. **Above and opposite:** The kitchen features an ambitious, yet very tightly curated mix of materials that includes the heavily figured marble of the island, enameled steel, wood, porcelain, lacquer, and the vibrant, Indian paintbrush–hued leather that covers the refrigerator door and connects the space to the living and dining areas.

Opposite: The primary bedroom, wrapped in textured wall covering and carpet the color of desert sand, also encompasses a stylish and quite distinctive work area for the lady of the house. Above: The spirited selection of fabrics celebrates somewhat unconventional colors that play off the various hues in the great room on the same floor. The furnishings also relate to those in the living spaces in terms of form, profile, and scale, as well as in the way they are energized by the choice of paintings.

Top: The main bathroom showcases the owners' love of unique figured stones. Left: The adjacent outdoor shower features a custom glass mosaic that celebrates the mountains that command the property's view. Opposite: The sumptuous, luminous onyx that forms the shower wall echoes the mesmerizing flow of falling water. The vibrant glass mosaic tile walls and countertops in the main bath bring in the accents of saturated aqua from the bedroom, providing a strong contrast that enhances both materials.

Opposite: One of the upstairs guest rooms serves first and foremost as a home office for the gentleman of the house. The custom lacquer and bronze partners' desk incorporates a rotating TV on a hydraulic lift for viewing while working or relaxing on one of the nearby daybeds. Above: The pair of day beds can comfortably accommodate overflow guests when necessary. The bright orange textiles and lacquer tie tightly to the playful series of "psychedelic" cowboy prints, a whimsical nod to the Southwest.

Above: The house is perfectly designed to facilitate the relaxed indoor/outdoor living that the climate in Paradise Valley makes possible. The backyard encompasses expansive terraces zoned for reading, conversation, dining, sunbathing, cooking, and media viewing. **Opposite:** One outdoor living area flows directly off its interior counterpart. **Following spread:** Multiple seating groupings and arrangements of various types surround the pool. An outdoor kitchen lives just a few steps up on another terrace.

Our view of the contemporary interior is not Bauhausian, straight-lined, or minimal. Although we occasionally nod to the strict, less-is-more dictum, our choices favor the embracing, the comforting, and the inviting. In conceiving each space, we visualize the desired experience from the moment of entry to the moment of exit with an eye to visual seduction. We determine the elements that will draw people in, where the loud statements should be, and where the whispers. Using a complex calculus of line, form, texture, color, finish, and function, we establish mood, atmosphere, a story line, romance—and ultimately rooms that want to be explored intimately.

Furnishings, materials, fabrics, finishes, objects, details, and art can and do exude mystery and allure. They entice and engage our senses and imaginations with character and personality. Some furnishings, those that are obvious abstractions of the human body, cannot help but beckon. Others command attention by their pure geometry of form. Still others seem to appear to strike a pose or manifest an attitude, be it sassy, pouty, perky, languid, and so on. Low-slung seating, for example, naturally invites the sitter to recline, to become a Madame or Monsieur Récamier for today. A giant double daybed, a tête-à-tête that allows for coupling, a voluptuously cushioned, all-embracing piece of upholstered furniture: each has an X-factor that can enhance the appeal of its neighbors, and the entire interior landscape.

Materials have their own qualities of seduction. Think of the endless variety of surfaces, the degrees of texture and finish that compel the hand to reach out and touch, and the body to engage. Contrasts may set off sparks of intrigue: the rough against the polished, the cool and shiny against the plush and deep, layer upon layer of texture, color, and sheen. A controlled swath of silk or satin on a bouclé that covers a sofa might brighten the fabric face, rather like lipstick. What could be more enveloping than a main bedroom with walls swaddled in luminous, silk velvet with just that touch of ombrage that speaks of repeated, easy engagement? Especially when that same silk velvet, now hand-painted with metallics of gold and silver to fool the eye, beckons at the windows while a deliciously deep wool-and-silk rug woven with gold thread entices underfoot.

Whether intense, rich, and saturated or very pale, ethereal, and soft, the extremes of tonality create their own style of embrace. The warmer end of the spectrum—the reds, oranges, and yellows—traditionally manifests as the psychological hot zone. The cooler side of the palette can generate a seriously sexy vibe, too. Dark maroon, midnight blue, forest green, deep dark moss: all the inky hues that transform rooms into caves evoke hidden depths. Then, of course, there is the chemical charge, the magnetism exuded when certain colors come together.

In interiors, complexity so often evokes sensuality because of the illusions and allusions it invokes, and the veiled messages it suggests. Sexy rooms inevitably live at a certain level of intrigue: dark spaces contrasting with light spaces, where the perimeters are unclear; delicately balancing the masculine and feminine, specifically the forms, shapes, textures, color palettes, materials, and details that we so often perceive in those terms. What does sexy mean in design? Rooms that instantly compel, that heighten the lived experience, but that only fully reveal their richness, depths, and complexities over time.

S E X Y

Pretty is a lovely thing, but sexy is a whole different adjective. Some like it hot. We absolutely do! Sinuous sensuality is a surefire way to infuse an interior with allure. Dark mirror, rippling onyx, a curvaceous sculpture or lush textile asking to be caressed, shades of the midnight hour—these are just some of the devices we put to work to seduce the eye.

GRAPHIC VISION

For people who love New York, views from on high inevitably quicken the heart. When the vantage point happens to be cloud-side in a sleek, next-generation, Midtown super-scraper, the uninterrupted panorama of Central Park and the peaks of Gotham's iconic skyline acquire an almost otherworldly quality. No wonder this expansive sky hold proved irresistible to this international family, who had long coveted a place in New York.

These clients have a deeply informed contemporary aesthetic, which in this case embraced a graphic approach to form and a black, white, and gray palette celebrating the breathtaking urban vistas beyond. Their preferences directed us toward a carefully curated minimalism, so we incorporated artisan pieces, vintage items, and statement furnishings in arrangements organized both to spotlight the standout designs and emphasize the views. As this design dialogue developed, it grew ever more elegant and refined through the contrast of forms, materials, and textures. We added spice with an occasional note of whimsy and focused on tonal depth to ensure the client's preferred urbane hues were just as interesting as they were unobtrusive.

The decorative voice started to emerge in the beautifully square foyer with walls finished in shagreen-embossed leather panels and a console of matte and polished bronze, one of several metals inserted as accents throughout. In the adjacent great room, versatility in function was key as these clients wanted the space to comfortably host a cocktail party for sixty just as easily as it provided a respite in the clouds for one or two. With that goal in mind, we organized the living area around a meandering seating group of back-to-back sectional sofas—one facing the media console and TV; the other, the view—arraying a suite of interesting chairs around the sofa's elements for various uses. By the window, we paired a chaise grouping with compelling sculptural pieces for scale to carve out a singular place for quiet contemplation or for a small cluster of friends during a party. Because of the open plan, it made sense to select a very long table in beautifully figured marble with chairs upholstered in horsehair to give the dining area its own gravitational pull. The kitchen was ample enough to encompass both a cozy breakfast area and a home office tucked to the side.

In the private cosmos of the main bedroom, the balance of the graphic palette naturally shifted toward the dark. Coal black walls made three-dimensional with horizontal incisions transformed this space with panoramic views into an embracing cave. Where better to contemplate the greatness of Gotham?

Page 238: The aesthetic directive prioritized bold forms and a sophisticated color palette built on urban contrasts. **Preceding spread:** The great room is a tasty recipe filled with statement pieces both contemporary and vintage, as well as site-specific custom designs. A very meandering main seating arrangement creates focus in multiple directions. **Opposite:** From materials to furnishings to art, each choice celebrates the city. **Above:** Predominantly black and white, the graphic palette radiates energy.

Above: The black-and-white palette runs throughout the apartment. The breakfast area, part of the kitchen, includes angular furnishings that are a response to the peaks, angles, and edges of the skyline that commands the view. Opposite: With rich accents of the deepest cobalt blue, the strict, chic, high-contrast palette works to profound dramatic effect to create this graphic vision in the dining room. The celestial motif in John Noestheden's triptych finds further expression in the ceiling fixture.

Preceding spread: The bedrooms are equally strong in presence. The main bedroom folds in medium-gray notes that resonate with the dominant black and white. A dollop of red introduces the spice that brings lingering heat into the mix. **Opposite and above:** In one of the two guest bedrooms, a softer tone takes over. Clean-line geometric furniture offers welcome and comfort. Vibrant emerald textiles not only delight the eye and the touch, they also make a connection to the great room's Central Park views.

L O F T
L I V I N G

As families grow, change beckons. It certainly did for this couple with two young children. After living in their Tribeca loft for some years, the two decided the time was ripe to reinvent it into the clean, contemporary, functional space they had long wanted, and the visual statement they truly desired. The program encompassed a new kitchen, primary bath, floors, and other significant requests; their sophisticated sensibility, knowledge of contemporary artisans, and interest in more than mere cosmetics, had us delve deep into our satchel of professional tricks—always a designer's treat.

The interior architecture reveled in the exposed structure of the nineteenth-century factory building. To soften the effect, we framed the large steel windows wrapping the living and dining areas, one of the apartment's great beauties, with curtain panels. We also painted the casements black to heighten the expression of the space's industrial origins.

For a tantalizing opening statement, in the entry we incorporated a pair of brooch-like sconces jeweled with smoky rock crystal orbs. The wide, tunnel-like hallway we put to work, inserting a lacquer paneled passage to create much-needed additional storage: think coat closets, pantries, and more. This revision also created a theater of release into the high-ceilinged public spaces.

The husband, a design aficionado always on the lookout, spotted the living room's mid-century lounge chairs online. They were in London, so on our next trip there, we sit-tested them, then shipped them home to be recovered in their vibrant cerulean velvet. Because the couple favors striking lighting, we commissioned contemporary ceiling fixtures for the adjacent living and dining areas; coated with a verdigris finish, the two similar forms took on a patina of the historic. For the dining room table, another commission, we selected a resin top with glints of suspended silver leaf to pick up on the surrounding metallics. Throughout, we emphasized textiles of delicious tactility.

In the kitchen we stepped out of the box, rotating L-shaped pieces of custom integrated cabinet hardware to create a Mondrian effect, a touch of lower Broadway Boogie-Woogie. The monolithic stainless-steel hood, conceived specifically to reflect light in all directions, provided quietude. As for the island, it was a eureka moment when the four of us came across its dramatically figured granite on a visit to the stone yard.

The primary bedroom carries through the notes of understated syncopation with an off-center furniture layout. Here, we continued the material choreography with velvet and hand-painted silvered panels, mottled suede walls, and moments of shagreen, bronze, and densely woven lurex. What could be more satisfying than to be the agents of such a change?

Page 250: This rock crystal sconce, one of a pair in the entryway, introduces a detail that bubbles up throughout. **Preceding spread:** The custom sofa opens its arms in a sweeping embrace expansive enough for the volume. The pendant light, one of two related designs commissioned from Lindsey Adelman, plays with the orb motif. **Top and right:** Sculptural pieces at various scales draw the eye. **Opposite:** Deep blues, tonal grays, and splashes of purple embellish the client's preferred black-and-white palette.

ENTRYWAYS OF MILAN   INGRESSI DI MILANO

JEAN MICHEL   FRANK

Opposite: The second commissioned pendant fixture crowns the adjacent dining area; its descending stems establish a degree of intimacy under the lofty ceilings. The chairs' exterior fabric subtly weaves in different threads of color from the surroundings. **Above left:** The dining table's custom resin top shimmers with suspended curls and arabesques of silver leaf. **Above right:** The client has a passion for unique objects. **Following spread:** The figured granite that clads the island provides durability and drama. Asymmetrical cabinetry hardware plays to the city's syncopated rhythms. A piece of functional sculpture, the custom hood casts dappled light around the room.

Left: From a bed wall enriched by velvet-upholstered panels flanked by glass panels of the same proportions to a plush rug with rivulets of Lurex, shagreen-covered vanity, and walls swathed in pearlescent paper, the primary bedroom incorporates an olio of luxurious and luminous materials. **Above:** The lacquered nightstands are custom made in two different widths to nest tightly into their corresponding bedside niches. A pair of quatrefoil rock crystal table lamps adds another glamorous embellishment.

Design has the uncanny ability to portray and encourage human connection, to use the inanimate to resonate with the animate. Our aim is to create spaces that allow a deeper relationship to others by capturing place, story, and time in a way that stimulates joy, compassion, and love while delighting the senses.

Our understanding of location and narrative tends to emerge through conversations in the early stages of the design process. These getting-to-know-each-other talks often elicit memories of places and experiences that spark love. Whatever the mementos of these happy times may be—the gold columns in the lobby of a favorite hotel, the specific architectural details so definitive of a particular place, a color that captivates in a foreign land—we find ways to integrate or translate them into the elements of design. We do this so that the finished rooms speak to heartfelt sensations and resonate with the realms that matter most to our clients, their family, and community, as well as their desire for restorative, spiritual, and creative time.

As we develop each program, we think about how these individuals wish to live and interact in each space. With proper planning, the same living room that allows for seamless entertaining can also accommodate areas for private introspection and intimate interactions with family and friends. A biomorphic swoop of a curvaceous sofa with seating pieces arrayed around it sketches out an embracing circle around the home fire and the groaning board, even if it is a low table. A grouping of four swivel chairs is conducive to quiet conversation.

Certain rooms inevitably emerge as stylish creative sanctuaries; dedicated spaces for meditation or yoga, for instance. So are dining rooms organized and furnished to do double service as art studios or crafting spaces with tables durable enough for a hot glue gun and other tools, and electrical outlets within easy reach. And we love *slumberlicious* bedrooms of all kinds: silk-velvet-swathed cocoons, luxuriously dark caves, glass boxes open to nature, or rooms that embrace the skyline yet are visually rooted to ground.

In our view, art and objects play uniquely powerful roles as affirmation. The paintings, sculptures, and objects that delight every day act as acknowledgments of accomplishment, as visually prominent versions of private personal mantras. Commissioning artisans who put care, intention, passion, and soul into their creations adds another form of vitalizing spatial energy. The two of us are often attracted to art that looks and feels celestial or oceanic, that transports its viewers into the vastness, expanding the confines of a room by suggesting the infinite. The natural and organic materials we favor—gorgeous marbles, onyxes, semiprecious stones, and such—reiterate this connection to pre-time and eternity, for they are both grounding and vast.

We certainly subscribe to the general notion that spaces have the power to calm and relax, to animate and inspire. We know that within one residence there can be many different moods. Design allows us to play with this idea ad infinitum. Creating beauty is a love language, after all, one of heart and best intentions where the practical meets the profound.

SPIRIT

To truly achieve a personal sense of place, a home needs this one vital, essential attribute: soul. We instill each space with spirit to evoke the seat of emotions and character. Flourishes and gestures such as custom mosaics and ceramic installations, a gilt-bronze bug, asteroids overhead, and moons rising and setting all lift our projects to another plane.

H O U S E
I N   T H E
W O O D S

Every project starts with a thousand questions. "Why?" is very often among the first. This couple, though, does things differently. At the time they unexpectedly happened upon this ode to the iconic glass houses of Ludwig Mies van der Rohe and Philip Johnson, a private oasis in New York State's Columbia County encompassing hundreds of acres of woods, we were in the middle of our fourth project together, a vast residence in Tribeca. For them, as with each residence we have completed together, the catalyst was, "Why not?"

The architect who designed the U-shaped house, which dates to 2007, incorporated every spatial device in the book to glorify the setting. The entrance deck opens to a fireplace wall and stair to the basement, a core of solidity amid the transparent structure. With separate wings for living areas and bedrooms, and a den bridged by the kitchen and dining area, the plan orchestrates a panorama that captures the surrounding wild and the changing seasons. At the time of purchase, the house was showing its age and in need of TLC, as well some general refinements and additional detail. To that end, we conceived a sensitive roof-to-slab renovation that was a restoration upward. We upgraded the kitchen and bathrooms, introduced state-of-the-art lighting and mechanical systems, and enhanced the materials palette with walnut and teak for floors, walls, ceilings, and millwork—sober and appropriate to the architect's original intent, yet still a rich contrast to the white-painted surfaces and restored concrete floors.

With this type of house, the interiors can skew far too easily into mid-century cliché. To avoid that, we opted to mix extremely contemporary pieces, many with references to nature, with custom items we designed and the very occasional element of mid-century modern for spice. To tie the interior and exterior together as seamlessly as possible, we selected materials that connect organically to the incredible natural world beyond the window walls. The tonalities throughout—deep forest hues of mushroom, bark, walnut, and oak—harmonize with the surroundings. Honed stone in the kitchen, for example, feels rich without being loud, the color of rocks tumbled in a stream. In the dining area, elements of high-gloss lacquer and polished metal interject touches of the urbane materiality we more typically deploy. Each selection, and the combination in its entirety, conveys the very tactile luxury that celebrates life's rich variety and yet still says "country house"—the "why" that answers the "why not?"

Page 268: A custom side-by-side partners' desk factors into each of this client's properties. Pages 270–271: The mission here was to create an interior that would not distract from the paradise outside yet be strong enough to have its own presence. Preceding spread: The living room furnishings address each other and the fireplace. Opposite: The space is outfitted for cozy conviviality. Above: Natural materials—wood, steel, shearling, ceramic, and others—come together to create interest in the living room.

On the books: JULIUS SHULMAN MODERNISM REDISCOVERED

Preceding spread: The front door opens directly onto the living room, where an inviting seating arrangement takes in both interior and exterior views. **Opposite:** The kitchen and dining wing extends on the opposite side of the courtyard. The dining area is raised a step for a subtle shift in perspective. **Top:** As throughout, these two areas embrace references to nature. **Left:** The round dining table is conducive to easy conversation.

Preceding spread: The main bedroom and its adjoining bath are truly tranquil retreats, yet quite sumptuous in their appointments and in the way they both open directly into the landscape. The bed rests against a wall-to-wall upholstered headboard that creates a grounding horizon line. **Opposite:** Luminous onyx and teak come together in the shower, tub, and vanity to create a room of exquisite simplicity. **Above:** Hand-woven textiles enrich the tightly curated mix of materials that dress the sleep chamber.

Above: The long hallway, raised a step from the living room, celebrates both the glory of the architecture and the exceptional beauty of the landscape that surrounds it. Opposite: This open space, with dark stained woods, textured organic fabrics, and a jute and wool rug that very consciously recalls a tatami mat, provides the owners with a Zen-like room of quiet comforts for peaceful, solitary contemplation that can easily be pressed into service as sleeping quarters for guests whenever the occasion arises.

ACKNOWLEDGMENTS

Working on this book has been a labor of love, a journey filled with memories of projects and, of course, the clients who allowed us the pleasure of getting to conjure up the realities they live in. We thank them immensely for their faith and trust.

We would also like to thank Philip Reeser, Ilaria Fusina, and Charles Miers of Rizzoli, whose enthusiasm and gentle editorial touches were instrumental in the end result. Judith Nasatir, our writer, who endured many, many, many meetings, always with joy and humor. Thank you for pulling all our thoughts and ramblings together with style and cohesion. Jill Cohen and Melissa Powell, wizards of the book world, who indeed are the place "Where Beautiful Books Begin" (to quote their website!). Sam Shahid, the emperor of graphic design, and his associate John MacConnell, for their elegant eye.

The photographers who captured our work so beautifully—without them there would be no BOLD—Stephen Kent Johnson, Joshua McHugh, Simon Upton, Brittany Ambridge, Trevor Tondro, Joe Schmelzer, and Marco Ricca. The suppliers, artisans, contractors, truckers, showrooms, workrooms, carpet installers, floor finishers, faux finishers, and on and on… the list of those we rely on to turn our visions into actuality is voluminous. Much gratitude and congratulations to each of you.

To our team at Drake/Anderson, past and present, all who have added so much to the projects included, your talents and input were essential. Cheers to you, Gustavo, Stella, Maryse, Vo, Dan, Ricardo, Tom, Sydney, Kelsey, Hong, Mark, Jenny, Elizabeth, Sally, Glenn, Allison, Paris, Amanda, Dounia, and Johanna. We thank you all immensely.

Our gratitude to all,
Jamie and Caleb

PHOTOGRAPHY CREDITS

Cover, 2, 4: Stephen Kent Johnson; 6: Joshua McHugh

Gotham Glamour: All images © Stephen Kent Johnson

London Calling: All images © Simon Upton

Exquisite
74: Simon Upton; 76 top left: Stephen Kent Johnson; top right: Marco Ricca; bottom: Brittany Ambridge; 77 top left: Stephen Kent Johnson; top right: Joshua McHugh; bottom left: Stephen Kent Johnson; bottom right: Joshua McHugh; 78-79: Brittany Ambridge

Forever Views: All images © Stephen Kent Johnson

Caleb's Apartment: All images © Stephen Kent Johnson

Confident
136: Brittany Ambridge; 138 top left: Joshua McHugh, top right: Marco Ricca, bottom: Joshua McHugh; 139 top left: Joshua McHugh, top right and bottom left: Brittany Ambridge, bottom right: Joshua McHugh; 140-141 Marco Ricca

Georgian Remix: All images © Joshua McHugh

An Ideal Aerie: All images © Marco Ricca

Witty
192: Stephen Kent Johnson; 194 top left and top right: Joshua McHugh, bottom: Stephen Kent Johnson; 195 top left: Stephen Kent Johnson, top right: Brittany Ambridge, bottom left and bottom right: Joshua McHugh; 196-197: Joshua McHugh

The Light Fantastic: All images © Brittany Ambridge

Desert Paradise: All images © Joe Schmelzer

Sexy
232: Trevor Tondro; 234 top left and top right: Joshua McHugh, bottom: Marco Ricca; 235 top left: Stephen Kent Johnson, top right: Marco Ricca, bottom left: Joshua McHugh, bottom right: Stephen Kent Johnson; 236-237: Stephen Kent Johnson

Graphic Vision: All images © Trevor Tondro

Loft Living: All images © Joshua McHugh

Spirit
262: Marco Ricca; 264 top left: Stephen Kent Johnson, top right: Marco Ricca, bottom: Stephen Kent Johnson; 265 top left: Joshua McHugh, top right: Joshua McHugh, bottom left: Trevor Tondro, bottom right: Joshua McHugh; 266-267: Brittany Ambridge

House in the Woods: All images © Stephen Kent Johnson

286: Marco Ricca

First published in the United States of America in 2022 by
Rizzoli International Publications, Inc.
300 Park Avenue South
New York, New York 10010
www.rizzoliusa.com

Publisher: Charles Miers
Editors: Philip Reeser and Ilaria Fusina
Production manager: Barbara Sadick
Design coordinator: Olivia Russin
Managing editor: Lynn Scrabis

Art Director: John MacConnell
DESIGNED BY SAM SHAHID

Developed in collaboration with Jill Cohen Associates, LLC

Copyright © 2022 by Drake/Anderson
Texts by Jamie Drake and Caleb Anderson with Judith Nasatir

ISBN: 978-0-8478-7243-5
Library of Congress Control Number: 2022931089
2022 2023 2024 2025 / 10 9 8 7 6 5 4 3 2 1
Printed in China

Facebook.com/RizzoliNewYork
Twitter: @Rizzoli_Books
Instagram.com/RizzoliBooks
Pinterest.com/RizzoliBooks
Youtube.com/user/RizzoliNY
Issuu.com/Rizzoli